All About Animals

Bears

By Catherine Lukas

Reader's Digest Young Families

Contents

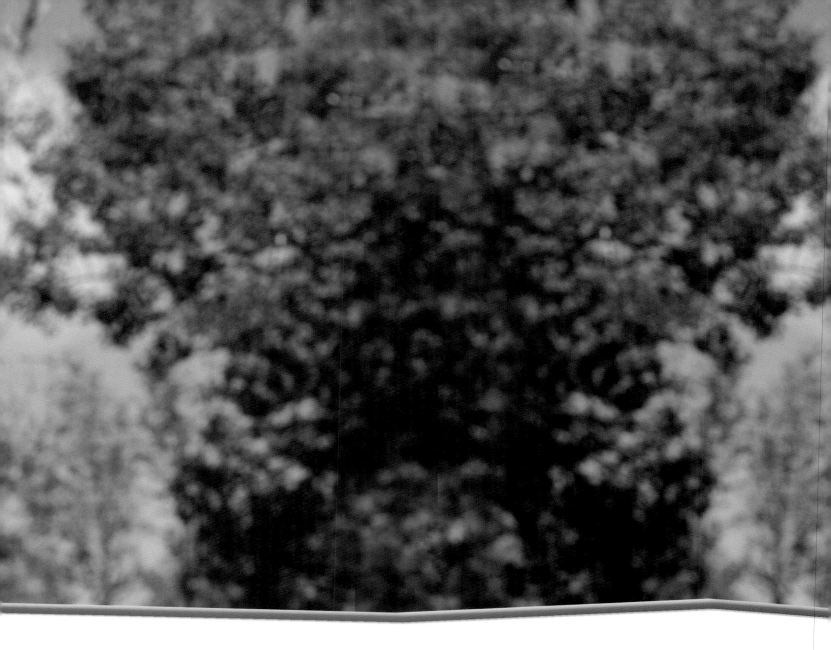

Chapter 1
A Bear Cub Grows Up

Sweet Tooth
Black bears like to lick sweet sap found underneath the outer layer of tree bark. The bears strip away the layer of bark with their teeth to get to the sapwood.

On a winter night inside her den, Mother Bear gives birth to Baby Bear. He is as tiny as a kitten and has hardly any fur yet! He nuzzles against his mother's soft fur, drinking her warm milk.

For two months, snow falls outside. While Mother Bear sleeps, Baby Bear drinks, sleeps, and grows. After four weeks, his eyes open and he is now covered with fur.

One day the bears are awakened by a steady dripping sound. The snow is melting. Baby Bear sniffs the warm spring air. Then he follows his mother out of the den. She moves slowly, as she has lost a lot of weight over the winter. It's time to eat!

Baby Bears

Baby black bears usually weigh less than a pound at birth! Hold a one-pound box of sugar in your hand to get an idea of how little this is!

Baby Bear watches his mother and quickly learns how to find food. He chews a stick, sniffing for ants and grubs to slurp up with his long, sticky tongue. He gobbles up sweet berries and nibbles on some wildflowers.

Mother Bear teaches him how to climb a tree. She knows he will be safe there while she hunts for food. The woods are full of dangers for little cubs. Wolves, mountain lions, and grizzly bears sometimes hunt for little bears. Safe and sound high in the tree, Baby Bear snacks on tasty leaves and takes a nap.

Suddenly Mother Bear rears up on her hind feet. She smells danger! She growls a warning, and Baby Bear watches from his perch.

It's a mountain lion! He stops when he sees Mother Bear towering over him, ready to fight. He scampers away quickly.

Little Bears
Baby bears weigh 4 to 8 pounds when they leave their den in the spring.

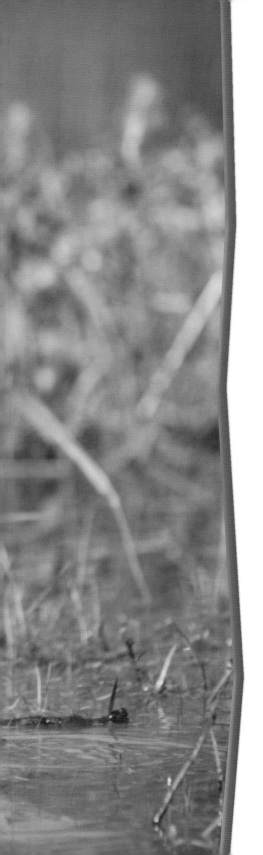

All summer and autumn, Mother Bear and her cub wander through the forests, eating as much as they can. She knows they must gain as much weight as possible to survive the coming winter. As the weather turns cold, Mother Bear searches for a new den for them to spend the winter. At last she spots the perfect place—a cave with a narrow opening.

Mother Bear and her cub prepare the den by dragging in and laying down soft moss and leaves for their beds. Then they snuggle together and begin their long rest.

When spring arrives, Baby Bear is almost a fully grown black bear. He will stay with his mother for a little while longer, and then, as all bears do, he will wander off to a different part of the woods to begin his own bear adventures.

Bear Beds

Many black bears prefer to sleep on soft beds for the winter rather than on bare cave floors. The bears build up their beds by bringing grass, leaves, moss, and bark into their dens.

Chapter 2
The Body of a Bear

Ghost Bears

One rare kind of black bear has white or cream-colored fur and lives off the coast of British Columbia in Canada. It is not a polar bear. Native Americans named these bears "ghost bears."

Which Bear?

The two most common types of bears are black bears and brown bears. In spite of their names, it isn't always easy to tell the difference. Not all black bears are black, and not all brown bears are brown! Black bears can be black, bluish black, chocolate brown, reddish, cinnamon-colored, tan, or even white! Some have a white V or patch of white fur on their chest.

Brown bears, including the grizzly, are usually brown, but the color of their fur ranges from tan to black. Grizzly bear fur is light at the end of each hair, which gives these bears a "grizzled" appearance.

Old Fur, New Fur

All bears shed their fur—called molting—once a year when their new fur grows in thickly for the winter.

To make identifying black and brown bears even more challenging, the fur color of some young bears can change as they get older. For example, a black bear can have brown fur for a while! Also, the fur of some bears darkens with time.

So how do you tell the difference between black and brown bears? One way is by their size—brown bears are bigger. Brown bears also have a hump on their shoulders. Their ears are short, round, and smaller than the ears of black bears. Brown-bear claws are longer and are a lighter color than those of black bears.

On the Move

Bears look large and sluggish, but they can run as fast as 30 miles per hour for short distances! That's faster than the fastest human sprinter!

While bears usually run and walk on all fours, they are able to stand upright on their back feet. They can walk in this position, but only for a few steps. Bears stand up to reach food, see into the distance, fight off an attacker, or sniff something interesting in the air.

Bears spend a lot of time on the move, searching for food, a mate, or a place to hibernate for the winter. They travel on remembered paths and will return to places that were good sources of food in the past. Bears will also explore new areas, especially when food is scarce.

Early Risers

Bears are the most active in the early morning and evening hours. During the summer and early fall, when they are storing up fat for their long winter's rest, bears may be active all day.

Strong Swimmers

Bears are good swimmers and like to be in the water. They go into the water to catch fish, cool off, escape pesky insects or a predator, and sometimes just for fun. Polar bears are the best bear swimmers. They can swim continuously for hours. Black bears can swim a mile at a time without stopping.

Despite their size, bears can run downhill, uphill, and sideways.

Just like people, bears are plantigrades. This means they walk by putting their entire foot flat on the ground, heel-first.

Paws and Claws

The claws of bears are curved, which gives these large animals surprising dexterity. Bears use their claws to turn over rocks and logs, pick berries from bushes, catch fish, and dig up roots to eat. The claws of black bears are so curved that they are able to open the lids of jars belonging to campers!

Sense of Smell

Most bears have good eyesight and hearing, but it's their sense of smell that is keenest. Bears can sniff out tiny insects inside logs or a dead animal a mile away! A bear's sense of smell is even better than that of a bloodhound!

Bears also use their sense of smell to communicate with one another. They leave their scent on trees and bushes to "tell" other bears they are in the area.

Climbing Trees

Black bears learn to climb trees when they are very young, and they soon discover how useful these plants are to them. Trees offer food (fruit, sweet sap, and insects), safety from predators, and branches for resting or play. Some bears even hibernate in the crook of a thick branch for the whole winter!

Adult grizzly bears don't climb trees, because they are too big and heavy, but their cubs do.

A black bear climbs by digging into a tree trunk with its front paws and then pushing up with its hind legs, like a giant caterpillar. It descends backward, hind legs first, much like humans do, by shimmying down feet first. Bears also slide down tree trunks or jump from low branches.

Smart Bears

Most bears are curious and quite intelligent. Bears will investigate new objects, noises, and smells to see if they are edible or simply interesting to play with. They have even outwitted humans who tried to prevent them from finding food in garbage cans and at campsites.

Bears also have very good memories. They can find their way to places where they previously found food—even places they have visited only once before! They remember paths and routes they've walked in the past and the locations of favorite dens.

Shy Bears

Both black bears and brown bears are easily frightened and naturally shy. However, mother bears, whether black or brown, are well known for their fierceness if their cubs are in danger.

Most brown bears avoid contact with people as much as possible, but some black bears live close to human populations.

Bears make a range of noises, including grunting, blowing, woofing, and growling. Cubs often whine or cry when they are upset or "chuckle" when they are happy.

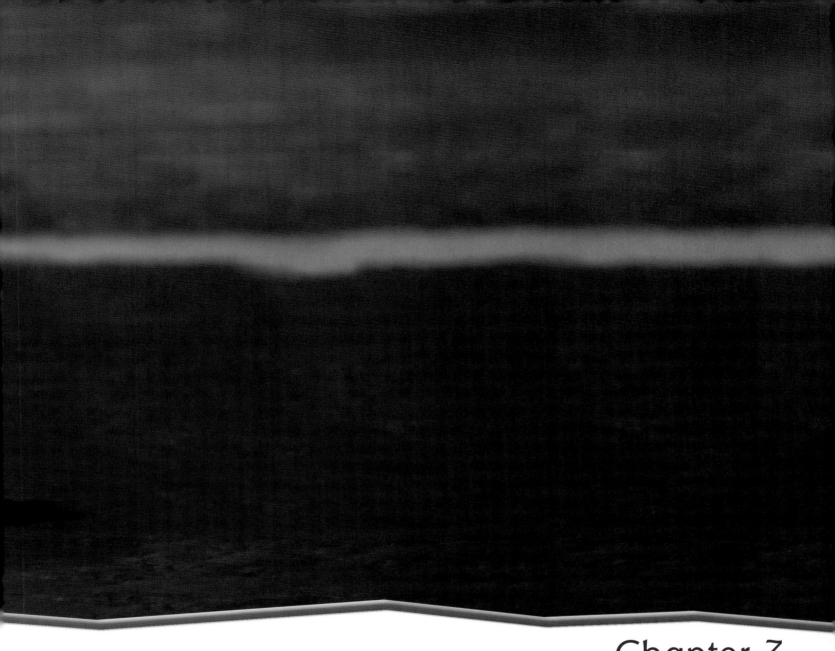

Chapter 3
Hungry as a Bear

Bear Teeth

Bears have 42 teeth; humans have 32. A bear's teeth are shaped for eating both plants and animals. The pointed front teeth catch hold of food, such as a squiggly fish, while the bear's flat molars work just like yours for crushing and grinding.

Although bears eat mostly plants, they love fish. Grizzlies are fond of salmon and wait at rivers to catch them. When salmon are plentiful, brown bears may eat up to 90 pounds a day!

Lunchtime All the Time!

Although scientists classify bears as carnivores, meaning "meat-eating" animals, bears are actually true omnivores—they eat both plants and animals. In fact, most of what they eat are plants. During the warm growing season, bears eat as much as 45 to 90 pounds of food per day!

A black bear uses its long, sticky tongue to help it collect tasty insects and lap up sweet sap from the inner bark of trees.

What do bears eat? Bears eat practically anything, but their favorite foods are fruit, nuts, acorns, greens, and insects. They also eat fish, small mammals, and honey! In some areas, brown bears hunt larger animals like moose, elk, and mountain goats. The type of food that bears eat can vary a great deal, depending on what region they live in and the time of the year.

Bears spend most of the spring, summer, and fall searching for and eating food in order to store as much fat as possible to get ready for winter hibernation.

Berry Picking

Black bears are not as clumsy as you might expect them to be. They can pick berries one at a time off bushes! They grasp and pull off the berries with their lips, which are very flexible. They also use their claws.

Ready for Winter

Bears are masters of survival. They have developed a perfect way to conserve energy during long harsh winters, when food is scarce. How do they manage this? By hibernating, which means sleeping all through the winter.

Bears hibernate in dens, which they begin to get ready in September or October. Bears choose many different kinds of places to build their dens, including caves, holes in the ground, or inside hollow logs. Sometimes they make their dens high up in a tree.

Some bears use the same den every winter. Others choose a new one every year.

During late summer and early fall, bears know they must gain as much weight as possible to get ready for the long winter. They eat as much as they can, day and night. Depending on the amount of food available, black bears at this time of year may gain 6 pounds a day. The extra fat nourishes bears during the long winter and helps keep them warm. As cold weather approaches, bears stop eating and grow more and more tired and sleepy.

Warm-weather Bears

Black bears that live in Florida and other southern states don't usually hibernate, although they often make a den and will sleep for periods of a few days during the "winter." A female black bear who is pregnant, however, will hibernate in the winter months.

Even though brown bears, like this grizzly, and black bears hibernate for the winter, they sometimes wake up and leave their dens for a little while to look for food in the snow.

During hibernation, a bear is nourished by the food it has stored inside its body. A bear who sleeps through the winter needs only one half the amount of oxygen required when it's awake and active.

The Big Sleep

In cold climates, bears sleep in their dens for as long as seven months—usually from mid-September to mid-April. The colder the winter, the longer the bears sleep. They fall into a deep sleep and do not eat, drink, or get rid of waste materials during this time. Sometimes bears wake up and emerge from their dens, but they come back soon to resume sleeping.

During hibernation, bears live off the body fat they stored up before the winter. When the weather warms up, usually in April or May, the bears come out of their dens. At first they are weak, having lost as much as half of their body weight. But as plants grow, the bears begin to eat and gain weight again and their energy returns.

A Long Winter's Nap

Some scientists believe that bears are not "true" hibernators, because their body temperature and heart rate do not drop significantly like those of other animals that hibernate. Some "true" hibernators—like ground squirrels and woodchucks—occasionally awaken, but go back into a deep sleep. Chipmunks, also "true hibernators," even go out, walk around, and eat.

Chapter 4
Bears and Babies

Mother bears teach their cubs how to find food and how to escape from predators. They are fiercely protective of their little ones and do not hesitate to attack if their cubs are in danger.

Mother Bears

Female black bears are ready to have babies when they are about five years of age. They give birth to cubs about every two or three years. Bears mate in May or June. The baby bear, however, does not begin to grow inside its mother until she has begun to hibernate, usually about November. Then its growth is fast—the bear cub is usually born in January or February, while the mother is hibernating. A mother bear generally gives birth to one to three cubs at a time, but scientists have recorded as many as six born to one mother.

Baby Bears Need Their Moms!

At birth, baby bears are tiny, toothless, and covered with wispy fur. They cannot see, hear, or smell until they are older. Baby bears are able to walk when they are five or six weeks old.

Baby Bears

When the mother bear gives birth to her cubs, she licks them and protects them by moving them next to her warm belly. As soon as they begin to nurse, she falls back into her deep sleep. The cubs continue to eat and sleep for two to three more months. The mother bear's milk is very high in fat, and the babies grow quickly. When spring arrives, they weigh from 4 to 10 pounds—about as much as a pet cat!

As soon as they emerge from their den, the mother bear teaches her cubs to find food. She shows them how to climb trees to avoid predators and, if necessary, rescues them from danger by carrying them gently in her mouth. In the fall of the cubs' first year, both mother and cubs help prepare a den for the winter. They then sleep snuggled together for warmth until the spring.

Not long after the cubs leave the den for the second time, at about 17 months of age, they are ready to leave their mother. But she may recognize her offspring for many years to come and allow them to search for food in her territory.

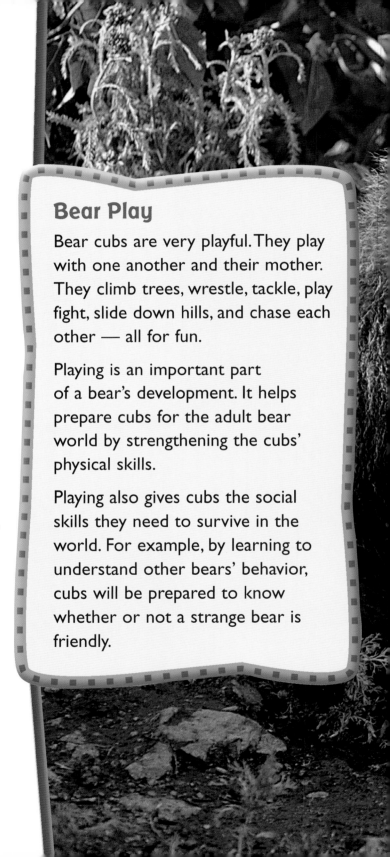

Bear Play

Bear cubs are very playful. They play with one another and their mother. They climb trees, wrestle, tackle, play fight, slide down hills, and chase each other — all for fun.

Playing is an important part of a bear's development. It helps prepare cubs for the adult bear world by strengthening the cubs' physical skills.

Playing also gives cubs the social skills they need to survive in the world. For example, by learning to understand other bears' behavior, cubs will be prepared to know whether or not a strange bear is friendly.

Bear moms and cubs are affectionate with one another. Bear cubs like to climb on their mom's back — for fun, comfort, or to get a better view!

Chapter 5
Bears in the World

Are Koalas Really Bears?

Koalas look so much like teddy bears that many people refer to them as koala bears. But koalas are not bears!

They are members of a special group of mammals called marsupials.

Marsupial moms have a built-in pouch for carrying their babies. Can you think of another marsupial that has a pouch? If you thought of a kangaroo, you are right!

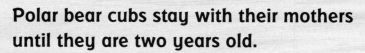
Polar bear cubs stay with their mothers until they are two years old.

All Kinds of Bears

There are many kinds of bears that live in different places around the world.

Black bears and brown bears live in North America. Some brown bears live in Europe.

Polar bears live where the climate is very cold—in the Arctic. They are the best swimmers of all the bears.

Spectacled bears get their name from the circles, which look like spectacles, around their eyes. These bears live in the Andes mountains of South America.

Sloth bears live in tropical and subtropical forests of India and Sri Lanka. They are slow movers.

Sun bears live in southeast Asian tropical and subtropical forests.

Panda bears live in China. They eat leaves from bamboo trees.

Bear Homes

Black bears and brown bears mostly live in forests. Often a bear's territory is not one large area but several smaller ones linked by pathways. Within its home range, a bear can travel to different habitats—from mountainside to berry patches to rivers with salmon.

All About Bears

Scientific name	Black bear	*Ursus Americanus*
	Grizzly bear	*Ursus arctos horribilis*
Order	Carnivora	
Family	Ursidae	
Size	Black bears	4 to 6 feet in length
	Grizzly bears	6 to 9 feet in length
Weight	Black bears	females average 150 pounds; males average about 285 pounds
	Grizzly bears	females range from 200 to 400 pounds;
	Grizzly bears	males range from 300 to 850 pounds
Life span	Black bears	up to 32 years in the wild
	Grizzly bears	25 to 30 years in the wild
Habitat	Black bears	forests, woodlands, swamps,
	Grizzly bears	mountain forests, tundra

The most important way to protect bears is by protecting and preserving their habitat so that the bears have plenty of room in which to roam.

The Future of Bears

Black bears and brown bears are not endangered, but other bears are at risk, especially giant pandas. The habitats of all bears are continually being threatened or shrunk by expanding human populations. The Arctic, where polar bears live, is in danger because of global warming.

Glossary of Wild Words

blubber   a thick layer of fat under the skin that keeps an animal warm and helps it float

buoyancy   the ability to float on, or rise to, the top of a liquid, like water

carnivore   a meat-eating animal

cub   a very young bear

den   a place where a wild animal rests or sleeps

edible   safe to eat as food

endangered   a species (a specific type) of plant or animal in danger of extinction

global warming   a rise in the average temperature of the earth's atmosphere

habitat   the natural environment where a plant or animal lives

hibernate   to go into a deep sleep all winter

mammal   an animal with a backbone and hair on its body that drinks milk from its mother when it is born

marsupial a kind of mammal whose mother carries her babies in a pouch

molars big teeth in the back of the mouth used for grinding food

molt to shed old fur, hair, or skin and have new fur, hair, or skin grow in

moss a small green plant that forms a soft mat on moist ground, rocks, or trees

nurse to feed a baby animal with milk from the mother's breast

offspring young animals that have the same mother

omnivore an animal that eats both plants and meat

predator an animal that hunts and eats other animals to survive

protein a substance found in all animals that is needed for growth and life

scent a smell left by an animal that other animals can identify

tundra a large plain in the Arctic with no trees

Index